CHRISTMAS
with
COUNTRY LIVING

Volume V

CHRISTMAS
with
COUNTRY LIVING™

Volume V

Oxmoor House®

HEARST COMMUNICATIONS, INC.

Christmas with Country Living™ Volume V
©2001 Hearst Communications, Inc., and Oxmoor House, Inc.
www.countryliving.com

Country Living™ is a trademark of Hearst Communications, Inc.
Oxmoor House, Inc.
Book Division of Southern Progress Corporation
P.O. Box 2463, Birmingham, AL 35201

ISBN: 0-8487-2437-2
ISSN: 1094-2866
Printed in the United States of America
First Printing 2001

Country Living™
Editor-in-Chief: Nancy Mernit Soriano
Art Director: Susan M. Netzel
Managing Editor: Mary R. Roby
Deputy Editor: Lawrence A. Bilotti
Senior Editor: Marjorie E. Gage
Senior Editor/Decorating & Design: Robin Long Mayer
Senior Editor/Special Projects: Marylou Krajci
Senior Editor/Home Building & Architecture: Pamela Abrahams
Editor/Food: Cynthia Nicholson

Oxmoor House, Inc.
Editor-in-Chief: Nancy Fitzpatrick Wyatt
Senior Editor, Copy and Homes: Olivia Kindig Wells
Senior Foods Editor: Susan Carlisle Payne
Art Director: James Boone

Christmas with Country Living™ Volume V
Editor: Susan Hernandez Ray
Associate Art Director: Cynthia R. Cooper
Designer: Clare T. Minges
Copy Editors: Donna Baldone, L. Amanda Owens
Copy Assistant: Jane Lorberau
Intern: Marye Binkley Rowell
Test Kitchens Staff: Gretchen Feldtman, R.D.
Assistant Foods Editor: Carolyn Land, R.D., L.D.
Illustrator: Kelly Davis
Senior Photographer: Jim Bathie
Director, Production and Distribution: Phillip Lee
Books Production Manager: Theresa L. Beste
Production Assistant: Faye Porter Bonner

Contributors
Guest Editors: Richard Kollath, Edward McCann
Editorial Contributors: Jan Hanby, Liz Seymour

WE'RE HERE FOR YOU!
We at Oxmoor House are dedicated to serving you with reliable
information that expands your imagination and enriches your life.
We welcome your comments and suggestions. Please write us at:
   Oxmoor House, Inc.
   Editor, *Christmas with Country Living*™
   2100 Lakeshore Drive
   Birmingham, AL 35209

To order additional publications, call 1-205-445-6560.

For more books to enrich your life, visit
oxmoorhouse.com

CONTENTS

$\mathcal{F}$OREWORD

Wreaths punctuated with holiday fruits, bowls enlivened with Christmas flowers, and treetops

frosted with snow—these are just some of the sights that make this season so beautiful. Come celebrate

all the wonders of Christmas in this edition of *Christmas with Country Living*.

Discover unique Christmas customs from various regions of the country. Go back in time and

enjoy the southern hospitality of Colonial Williamsburg (pages 14–29); the elaborate outdoor swags and

wreaths seen there are inspired by the embellishments of the 1700s. Incorporate combinations of fruits,

greens, and other naturals into your own holiday adornments. Get inspiration from the Adirondack style

of decorating enjoyed in New York State's northerly mountains (pages 68–77). Visit two hotels in Yosemite

National Park (pages 78–115), where the ornaments, the garlands, and the centerpieces reflect the history

of the area.

If it's a simpler holiday you're looking for this year, remember there's no greater joy than spend-

ing the holidays at home. Bring the joys of the season into every room with some of our ideas for quick

and easy arrangements (pages 32–35). Then greet guests—and family members—with batches of our

homebaked goods (pages 130–149).

However you decide to celebrate, we wish you a happy holiday season.

THE EDITORS OF *COUNTRY LIVING*

AMERICAN TRADITIONS

COLONIAL WILLIAMSBURG

ON THE FIRST SUNDAY IN December, the town of Williamsburg dons its fancy dress of holly, pine, mistletoe, magnolia, and mountain laurel garlands. Elaborate groupings of fresh fruits that celebrate the colors of the season punctuate these natural decorations. That evening, candles are lit in the historic area. On a more spectacular scale, the Grand Illumination lights up the sky with old-fashioned white fireworks, sparking Colonial Williamsburg's month-long Christmas celebration.

In the 1700s this season of Southern hospitality, well-known even back in England, was filled with wonderful feasts that coincided with balls, foxhunts, and winter weddings. Shopwindows were covered with ads for such popular presents as little books and sweets for children. Other gift-giving traditions from Europe followed, including the custom of jolly St. Nicholas filling children's wooden shoes with fruits and candies. Today, visitors can relive the splendor of Christmas in Colonial Williamsburg with tours and events hosted by costumed reenactors.

The Governor's Palace (above) is located at the end of the Palace Green. The original palace was completed in 1722 under Governor Spotswood. Opposite: Guides in period costumes lead daily tours that feature the decorations.

Expensive and rare fruits, imported from the West Indies, were an integral element of the Christmas decorations in Williamsburg. Colonial homes reflect this custom with their intricately designed embellishments. The fan-shaped arrangement over the door and the swags underneath the windows gleam with bright red apples. A pineapple, considered the traditional symbol of welcome, highlights the over-the-door adornment.

Classic Colonial Williamsburg decorations shine during the otherwise bleak days of winter. Many visitors return to Williamsburg each year to delight in new combinations of materials and to gain inspiration for their own homes. A charming circle of greenery, red and green apples, and red berries hangs on a wrought iron rail to greet guests (above). Opposite: A grid of apples and oranges set against a green backdrop adds a bold holiday touch to a front door. Smaller arrangements of fruits and greens flank the door, and above it an elaborate fan of fruits, greenery, and plumes surround the hospitable pineapple (top). Leaves, apples, and pinecones simply and beautifully grace a windowsill (bottom).

FRUIT FAN

1 To make this decoration, you will need a piece of plywood cut to the desired shape and size, a hammer, nails, a staple gun and staples, magnolia leaves, a pineapple, lemons, red apples, and boxwood. Referring to the photos above, hammer the nails in rows into the plywood.

2 Starting at the top, staple magnolia leaves to cover the plywood entirely.

3 Press the pineapple onto nails at the center of the plywood. Press the lemons onto nails around the top and the bottom of the plywood.

4 Press the apples onto the remaining nails on the plywood. Fill any gaps with magnolia leaves and boxwood.

Much loved for its beauty, taste, aroma, and healthy properties, the humble orange has found a place in holiday decorations around the world. Here, it serves as a glowing centerpiece for a swag of greens, red berries, nuts, and pinecones (above, left). Pomegranates, lemons, and naturals surround a pineapple (above, right), one of many exotic fruits imported to Colonial Williamsburg. Opposite: Pinecones and pods add unusual textures to a ring of greenery punctuated with red apples.

Apples, lemons, pods, and greenery (above and opposite) are some of the numerous materials used as Christmas embellishments in Colonial Williamsburg. Other fruits available to Virginians at the time included lady apples, limes, cranberries, and oranges. Berries, such as holly berries, chinaberries, rose hips, beauty berries, and bittersweet berries, were also popular. Additional favorite items were dried flowers, okra pods, lotus pods, dried cayenne peppers, and milkweed pods.

Pineapple

A N   E S S A Y

he people of central Brazil and Paraguay called the pineapple *nana* or "excellent fruit." Hundreds of years after it was first tasted by Europeans, the pineapple remains one of the most excellent products of the plant kingdom. Prickly on the outside, exploding with sweetness on the inside, it is unlike any other fruit that sets the holiday table. Its historical roots stretch back to the lush lowlands of South America; from there it traveled to the islands of the Caribbean, where Columbus first encountered the pineapple on his second voyage to America.

The spiny fruit, with its jaunty cockade of leaves, was much loved by the West Indians, who would place fresh pineapples at the entrances to their villages to indicate a welcome to visitors. Carried across the ocean to Europe, the pineapple became the delicacy of kings—considered so rare and precious that Charles II of England commissioned a portrait of himself receiving a pineapple as a gift. By the end of the sixteenth century, traders and explorers had introduced the pineapple to nearly every tropical region of the earth, and its cultivation spread from Africa to India to the South Sea islands.

The pineapple holds special meaning in American holiday traditions. Entertaining was an important part of the household life of the American colonies, especially in the South, where villages were widely scattered and inns were few and far between. Housewives set their tables with elaborate displays of sweets and fruits to welcome guests at holiday times. The exotic pineapple, rare and expensive in the days of slow-sailing ships, held pride of place (less wealthy Colonists would sometimes rent pineapples for the evening to dress up their tables). Often, a returning sea captain would hang a pineapple on his front gate to signal that he was home from his journey and ready to receive visitors. Determined householders—George Washington among them—even managed to cultivate the exotic fruit in their greenhouses.

Associated with generosity and good cheer in North America—as in the West Indies—the pineapple became a natural symbol of hospitality, reproduced in everything from quilts to weathervanes to bedposts as a sign of welcome. Today, whether it is fresh or candied, real or represented in brass or china, the pineapple still says "Welcome, we're glad you're here."

An Apple Cone (left), available from Williamsburg, can be used to create a variety of fruitful topiaries (see Resources on page 154). Simply arrange magnolia or similar leaves on a round piece of cardboard; then place the cone on top of the leaves. Starting at the base, and placing the largest pieces at the bottom, press the desired fruits onto the nails in horizontal rows. Fill in with greenery. A pineapple tops each of these festive little trees: covered with lemons, berries, and variegated greens, with the brown sides of the leaves as a base (below, left); punctuated with apples and greenery sprigs (below, right); and accented with pomanders and boxwood (opposite).

SIMPLE
PREPARATIONS

ARRANGEMENTS

FRESH FLOWERS IN THE MIDDLE of winter are a wonderful gift—whether to a friend or to yourself—filled with the promise of sunnier days to come. An alternative to perishable cut stems are these economical, long-lasting arrangements composed of living plants. The variety of blooms seen in these groupings were purchased in three-inch pots.

Holiday decorations let you create lovely combinations of the familiar and the new—and often give you the opportunity to see familiar things with new eyes. It is a particular pleasure at Christmastime to take out a favorite vase—or even a pitcher or a basket that is used for ordinary household tasks—and fill it with aromatic fresh flowers and greens. With so many lovely blooms available year-round these days, you can enjoy the luxury of mixing up the seasons: a branch of springlike azaleas or summery rosebuds combined with pinecones and sprigs of evergreen or fruits and seedpods. It is easy to add variety to the traditional holiday palette of red and green with inventive and even unexpected materials that put a personal stamp on Christmas decorating.

A simple footed bowl (above) becomes a pedestal for beautiful and inventive holiday arrangements (opposite and following pages). Silvered pinecones are tucked into a loose arrangement of snowy azaleas offset with dusty miller.

Almost any leakproof container will work for an arrangement, as long as it has a large reservoir for water and a wide mouth to hold flowers without crowding. Consider both line and mass when selecting the elements for an arrangement: vertical stems give the grouping height, and a combination of full flowers or greenery and smaller touches—tiny flowers, foliage, or seed heads—fill out the shape. Add a bit of imagination and whimsy—and enjoy the arrangement all season long.

A tiny spruce and a spray of cyclamen blossoms are skirted with moss and ornaments (above). Opposite: Miniature roses continue to grow surrounded by bright green limes, gilded pinecones, and seeded eucalyptus.

Christmas Candy

AN ESSAY

rightly colored, fancifully shaped, and beautifully presented, hard candy is as satisfying to the eye as it is to the taste. It is an integral part of the holiday season, whether tucked into a stocking on Christmas morning, heaped in a crystal dish on a sideboard, or attached to a home-made gingerbread house with icing.

In the midst of our modern abundance, it is difficult to believe what a rare treat sweets were even a few generations back. During the Depression a penny would buy a piece of gum, a paper of candy buttons, or a stick of licorice—but pennies themselves were hard to come by.

Centuries ago candy was reserved solely for special occasions. Until the Renaissance, when international trade made cane sugar widely available in Europe, any kind of sweets was precious. In fact, until the fourteenth century candy was used mostly medicinally, to hide the bitter taste of remedies, and was distributed by physicians. Though by the seventeenth century hard candy was available as a special treat, it was not until 1851 that a display of hard candy—"boiled sweets" in British parlance—at the Crystal Palace Exhibition in London ushered in the modern confectionery industry and put penny candy on the counters of general stores.

Confectioners make a distinction between soft candy—everything from fudge to nougats—and hard candy. Virtually all candy is made by dissolving sugar in water and boiling; as sugar passes through different temperatures, it changes its crystalline structure. Therefore, hard candy is nothing more than sugar water boiled until its moisture content has been reduced to 2 percent or less. Brittle and susceptible to moisture, the best hard candy is not meant to be kept for long—and seldom is!

Those candies that appear only at certain times of the year—such as chocolate Easter eggs and Halloween candy corn—stand out in our memories. Satiny ribbon candy is all the sweeter for its warm associations with Christmas. Laborious to make (classic ribbon candy is shaped by hand on a cool marble slab), ribbon candy holds an honored place among the Christmas candies. Ribbon candy, along with licorice, gum drops, and peppermints (opposite and following pages), adds to the season's festivities.

A MERRY
CHRISTMAS

With friendly thoughts at Christmas
With warm remembrance, too.
And wishes that the New Year may
Be very good to you.

A snowy, cheery, old fashioned
MERRY CHRISTMAS

Good Luck for X mas

Best Wishes
for a merry Christmas

A MERRY
CHRISTMAS

Hearty Greeting – just to say–
I wish you joy on Christmas Day!
A host of joys I'm wishing you,
So may my wishes all come true.
A Merry Christmas.

A Merry
Christmas

With
best
Wishes
for
Christmas

 POSTCARDS

THE TRADITION OF SENDING written wishes for a joyous holiday season to friends and family began centuries ago. But at the beginning of the 1840s, Sir Henry Cole found himself too busy to send personal letters, so he hired artist John Callcott Horsley to design a printed postcard for him. Soon a thousand of these cards went on sale for a penny apiece in London stores.

By 1907 printed postcards had grown in popularity in America. Beautifully illustrated, Christmas scenes were the main theme of these mistletoe- and holly-trimmed cards, many of which were issued in a series. Such elaborately designed postcards gave way in the 1920s to mass-produced cards, whose style favored natural lines and muted colors. Most depicted children, New England churches, horse-drawn stagecoaches, and nativity scenes.

The modern Christmas card emerged around 1930, when folded cards became the typical greeting form. Over the years, the themes have evolved to produce the variety of cards available today.

Christmas cards of the early 1900s reflected many Victorian themes (above, opposite, and following pages). These single-sided cards with simple messages were either mailed or used as calling cards. Collectors can still find a wide variety of illustrations and styles of Christmas postcards.

With Best Christmas Wishes

Alla

A Happy New Year

GOOD LUCK AT CHRISTMAS
May Happiness attend you
As Xmas-tide draws near,
And all you wish await you
Throughout the coming year.

A merry Christmas

A Joyful Christmas to You

HELLO, FOLKS!
A MERRY CHRISTMAS TO YOU ALL

Christmas Greetings

25 December

A Merry Christmas

Wishing you a Merry Christmas

A Happy Christmas

Christmas Greetings

A Merry Christmas

Christmas Wishes With Love

Christmas Greetings

A Merry Christmas

Wishing you a Merry Christmas

Dreams of Santa Claus

CANDLE RINGS

CHRISTMAS MEMORIES ARE BATHED in candle glow. From a pillar in the window on a frosty night to tapers on the holiday table on Christmas Eve, candles are an inseparable element of the season. Candles are even more festive when they rise from circles of greenery and flowers. An inexpensive ring of florist's foam—available in sizes designed for both pillars and tapers—is the foundation for this look. Soak in water and fill with fresh cuttings, or leave as is and decorate with pretty dried materials. A simple candle ring can turn almost any candlestick or flat container—or even a bare tabletop—into a unique and lovely display.

Candle rings can be custom-made to coordinate with various styles of holiday embellishments. Experiment with ring arrangements: combine cuttings from the yard with sprigs of flowers clipped from indoor plants or tuck unusual materials into the mix for unexpected color and texture. With a few natural additions, the humble candle ring offers beauty that belies its simplicity and low cost.

A handsome antique tree stand is transformed into a candleholder with the simple addition of a pillar candle and a candle ring made of florist's foam (above). Opposite: Filled with seeded eucalyptus, the candle ring surrounds the glowing candle with a seasonal skirt of greenery.

Supported on an antique tree stand, a white candle nestles in a simple arrangement of azalea blossoms and variegated petisforum (above, left). An aromatic beeswax pillar is set on a tabletop and dressed up with a ring of cedar, dried roses and larkspur, white berries, bunny tails, and cotton pods (below, left).
Opposite: A silvery cake stand does double duty as a candleholder and container for a delightful grouping of miniature roses, galax, and dusty miller.

THISTLE RING

1 To make the wreath, you will need a foam ring, thistle, and galax leaves. Soak the foam ring in water for at least an hour.

2 Cut the thistle and galax leaf stems to the desired length and insert them into the ring. To keep the wreath fresh longer, simply soak it in water every few days. It will also dry beautifully, providing a great-looking ring that will last all winter.

STATICE WREATH

1 To make the wreath, you will need a foam ring, statice, and a hot-glue gun and glue sticks.

2 Hot-glue bunches of statice around the foam until the wreath is completely covered. This wreath will last indefinitely if you keep it away from direct sunlight so that the flowers won't fade.

Pepper berries decorate the top of a container holding a brilliant blooming azalea (above). Small pots of white poinsettias grace a basket filled with pepper berries, orange pomanders, and pinecones (opposite).

Preceding pages: Accented by orange kumquats and red miniature roses, a forest of evergreens combines with birds' nests and golden glazed ceramic pineapples to create an inviting display.

SIMPLE FARE

GINGER-PUMPKIN SOUP

(PICTURED ON FACING PAGE)

YOU CAN PREPARE THIS SOUP SEVERAL DAYS AHEAD AND STORE, REFRIGERATED, IN AN AIRTIGHT CONTAINER. WHEN READY TO SERVE, SLOWLY WARM OVER LOW HEAT.

MAKES 10 SERVINGS

2 15-ounce cans pumpkin purée
3 14½-ounce cans chicken broth
1 11.5-ounce can pear nectar
⅓ cup creamy peanut butter
2 cloves garlic, finely chopped
2 tablespoons grated fresh ginger
2 tablespoons finely chopped green onion
1 tablespoon fresh lime juice
½ teaspoon salt
¼ teaspoon ground cayenne pepper

1. In a 6-quart saucepan, combine pumpkin purée, chicken broth, and pear nectar. Bring to a boil over high heat. Cover, reduce heat to low, and simmer 10 minutes.

2. In a blender or the bowl of a food processor fitted with chopping blade, process 1 cup pumpkin mixture with peanut butter until smooth. Return to saucepan with the remaining pumpkin mixture. Add garlic, ginger, green onion, lime juice, salt, and cayenne pepper; cook 10 minutes over medium heat.

3. Divide soup among mugs or soup bowls. Serve the soup immediately.

•NUTRITION INFORMATION PER SERVING—PROTEIN: 4G; FAT: 1G; CARBOHYDRATE: 13G; FIBER: 2G; SODIUM: 523MG; CHOLESTEROL: 0.5MG; CALORIES: 71

PROSCIUTTO-PROVOLONE HERO

MAKES 4 SERVINGS

PESTO:
½ cup fresh basil
¼ cup fresh parsley
2 tablespoons finely grated Parmesan cheese
1 tablespoon pine nuts
2 tablespoons olive oil
1 clove garlic
⅛ teaspoon ground black pepper

SANDWICH:
1 15-inch loaf Italian bread
2 cups spinach leaves, stemmed
½ pound sliced provolone cheese, each slice cut in half
¼ pound thinly sliced prosciutto
¼ pound thinly sliced hard salami or cappicola or a mixture of the meats
Garden vegetable pickles (optional)

1. Prepare Pesto: In the bowl of a food processor fitted with chopping blade, process first 7 ingredients until a paste consistency.

2. Assemble Sandwich: With a serrated knife, cut bread horizontally in half. With fingers, remove soft bread from the center of each half, leaving ½-inch-thick crust. (Freeze leftover soft bread for stuffing or bread crumbs.)

3. Spread cut surfaces of bread with Pesto. Cover bottom half of bread with spinach leaves and overlapping halved slices of provolone cheese. Add prosciutto and salami and cover with top of bread. Cut crosswise into 4 sandwiches. Transfer sandwiches to a serving plate. Serve with pickles, if desired.

•NUTRITION INFORMATION PER SERVING WITHOUT PICKLES—PROTEIN: 45G; FAT: 38G; CARBOHYDRATE: 68G; FIBER: 3G; SODIUM: 2,563MG; CHOLESTEROL: 91MG; CALORIES: 804

MAPLE POPCORN

TWO NATIVE NEW WORLD FOODS COMBINE TO MAKE THIS TEMPTING SNACK. SERVE THIS TREAT SHORTLY AFTER IT'S MADE, WHILE AT ITS CRISPY BEST.

MAKES 6 SERVINGS

⅓ cup unpopped popcorn
⅔ cup sugar
⅔ cup water
⅛ teaspoon cream of tartar
⅔ cup maple syrup
2 tablespoons butter
½ teaspoon salt

1. Pop popcorn in a hot air popper into a large bowl. Generously grease a baking sheet; set aside.

2. In a 2-quart saucepan, heat sugar, water, and cream of tartar to a boil over high heat, stirring occasionally. Brush side of pan with warm water to dissolve crystals forming at edge. Reduce heat to medium and continue cooking without stirring until mixture becomes deep golden brown—about 10 minutes.

3. Carefully stir in maple syrup and cook 2 minutes longer. Remove from heat and stir in butter and salt until butter melts. Immediately pour sugar mixture over popcorn; with long-handled spoon, carefully stir popcorn to coat with sugar mixture. (Do not use hands; syrup is very hot.) Pour all onto greased baking sheet to cool. Serve when cool or store in an airtight container up to 2 days.

•NUTRITION INFORMATION PER SERVING—PROTEIN: 1G; FAT: 4G; CARBOHYDRATE: 49G; FIBER: 1.0G; SODIUM: 216MG; CHOLESTEROL: 10MG; CALORIES: 232

TRAIL MIX

(PICTURED ABOVE)

MAKES 10 SERVINGS

1 cup cashews
1 cup dried apricots, quartered
¾ cup walnut halves
½ cup shelled sunflower seeds
½ cup golden raisins
⅓ cup dried cranberries
½ cup sugar
1 teaspoon 5-spice powder
¼ teaspoon ground cinnamon
½ teaspoon salt
1 large egg white
1 teaspoon water

1. Heat oven to 225°F. In a large bowl, stir together cashews, apricots, walnut halves, sunflower seeds, raisins, cranberries, sugar, 5-spice powder, cinnamon, and salt. Beat the egg white and water until frothy and fold gently into fruit-nut mixture.

2. Spread mixture out onto a nonstick baking sheet and bake 1 hour. Cool on baking sheet on a wire rack and break apart into pieces. Store in an airtight container.

•NUTRITION INFORMATION PER SERVING—PROTEIN: 5G; FAT: 13G; CARBOHYDRATE: 26G; FIBER: 2.0G; SODIUM: 117MG; CHOLESTEROL: 0MG; CALORIES: 236

Bejeweled Popcorn Balls

(PICTURED ABOVE)

MAKES 16 POPCORN BALLS

3 tablespoons vegetable oil, divided

12 cups popped popcorn (about ¾ cup unpopped)

2 cups golden raisins

2 cups dried cranberries

1¼ cups sugar

¾ cup firmly packed light brown sugar

1 cup light corn syrup

½ cup water

1 tablespoon lemon juice

1. Prepare the work area: In a large bowl lightly coated with 2 tablespoons oil, combine the popcorn, raisins, and cranberries. Use 2 teaspoons oil to lightly oil a long fork or spoon. Next to the bowl, place 2 trays lined with waxed paper.

2. Make the syrup: In a medium saucepan with a candy thermometer attached, place the sugars, corn syrup, water, and lemon juice. Place over medium-high heat and bring to a boil. Reduce heat to medium and continue to cook until the syrup reaches the hard ball stage (260°F). Remove from heat.

3. Make the popcorn balls: Pour the syrup over the popcorn mixture, using the fork to toss the popcorn and evenly distribute the syrup. Cool the popcorn for 1 minute and rub hands with remaining teaspoon of the vegetable oil. Use your hands to form 3-inch-wide balls and place on the lined trays. Cool completely. Store in an airtight container.

•NUTRITION INFORMATION PER POPCORN BALL—PROTEIN: 1G; FAT: 3G; CARBOHYDRATE: 71G; FIBER: 2.0G; SODIUM: 32MG; CHOLESTEROL: 0MG; CALORIES: 303

CEDAR STARS

1 To make these rustic stars, you will need the pattern on page 156, tracing paper, a pencil, a craft knife, cardboard, fishing wire, scented cedar, and raffia.

2 For each, use the tracing paper and the pattern to transfer the star pattern onto the cardboard; cut out. Use the fishing wire to attach bunches of cedar to the star.

3 Once the star is covered with cedar, wrap the star with raffia; knot the raffia in back to secure. If desired, use duct tape to attach a stick to the back of the star; press the stick into a container filled with florist's foam.

GOLDEN PINECONE

1 To make this golden decoration, you will need gold spray paint, a sugar cone (see Resources on page 154), assorted miniature pinecones on sticks, florist's foam, a container, florist's picks, and greenery.

2 Spray-paint the sugar cone and the pinecones gold; let them dry. Place the florist's foam inside the container. Attach a florist's pick to the bottom of the sugar cone and press it into the center of the florist's foam.

3 Cut the greenery to the desired length and press it into the florist's foam at the base of the sugar cone. Fill in with the miniature pinecones, pressing the picks directly into the florist's foam. (You may also use plain pinecones by wrapping them with the wire ends of florist's picks.)

Create an easy and portable centerpiece by bundling
dried lavender and red and white berries and then
placing them in a footed bowl. Punctuate the center
of the arrangement with a small pinecone. The sooth-
ing lavender not only looks great, but also adds its
pleasing fragrance to the room.

HOLIDAY
DESTINATIONS

AN ADIRONDACK CABIN

WINTER COMES EARLY AND lingers long in New York State's northerly Adirondack Mountains. Lakes that were active with boats and swimmers in the summer now lie still under a thick layer of ice. Cold mornings are scented with balsam and wood smoke, as the shadows under the trees turn from black to blue. The only sound is the swish of a cross-country skier traversing the expanse of a snowy field. Hushed and snowbound, the world pauses.

Adirondack style has spread far beyond the upper reaches of New York State, but there's still no better place to experience its unique charm than in those mountains themselves. Suspended in time, the villages and the inns of the Adirondacks recall the unhurried days of rambling camps and lodges, a period when city dwellers could escape to the mountains for leisurely vacations that might last a month or even a season. Christmas in the Adirondacks is a time for riding in a sleigh or skiing (some parts of the region receive as much as 300 inches of snow during the winter), trimming an aromatic tree, or dozing away a long winter evening in front of a wide stone fireplace.

A freshly cut tree (above) is trimmed with miniature snowshoes, souvenirs made in the 1930s and 1940s by Maine's Penobscot and Canada's Micmac people. Opposite: The lofty living room in a house near Lake George, New York, is decorated in rustic style with woven backpack baskets, rough-hewn log furniture, and Navajo rugs.

Winter sports have become increasingly popular in the Adirondacks since the Winter Olympic Games were held in Lake Placid in 1932 and 1980. Skiers and sledders can take a break at one of the many trailside inns in the Adirondack villages, making the mountains a favorite destination for Christmas vacationers. Sightseers also enjoy exploring the old towns and the beautiful scenery that the mountains have to offer. Backpack baskets (above and opposite) are great carriers for short daytime exploring trips, in addition to making beautiful containers for holiday naturals (see Resources on page 154).

A swag of greenery drapes from a caribou antler banister
with applewood posts (above and preceding pages) in an
Adirondack cabin. Opposite: Greenery hangs from the
chandelier over a table set with picture frames that feature dinner guest's photos. Rattan-seat chairs built in the
1930s by Indiana's Old Hickory Chair Company team up
with a 1920s table crafted by North Carolina's Reverend
Ben Davis.

A pair of Adirondack prints hangs over a side table decorated with Christmas greens, pinecones, and limes (above). Opposite: Late-1800s fishing creels, bark-and-twig frames made by Native Americans in the twentieth century, and moose carved in New Hampshire in the late 1800s populate cedar shelves accented with greenery.

Yosemite: The Ahwahnee

In 1890 President Theodore Roosevelt officially signed Yosemite National Park into being, thus preserving a 1,500-square-mile section of the Sierra Nevada of central California. John Muir, founder of the Sierra Club, once called this area "a landscape . . . that after all my wanderings still appears as the most beautiful I have ever beheld." A rich scenery of alpine meadows, broad valleys, and mountains, the park includes spectacular waterfalls, groves of ancient sequoias, and deep, clear lakes, untouched in a natural wilderness area.

Over four million people come to Yosemite every year, but in the middle of winter, when the valleys and the mountains are accented with snow, the stream of visitors slows to a trickle. Those that do come find a transformed landscape of snowy trails crisscrossed with tracks of pine martens and field mice. At night, under a high sky dense with stars, coyote calls echo across frozen lakes. Inside one of Yosemite's historic lodges, winter is greeted with a round of workshops and seminars on everything from snowshoeing to photography. Muffled in snow and silence, Yosemite becomes a place of timeless enchantment.

Topiary deer with cast resin antlers (above and opposite) graze in front of The Ahwahnee, whose name is derived from the Native American word for Yosemite Valley (see Resources on page 154 for topiary forms). The historic 123-room hotel, built in 1927, remains one of the most distinctive and elegant hotels in America. Following pages: A view from The Ahwahnee.

Geometric disks and diamonds, dotting a garland (above) and a
Christmas tree (opposite), were inspired by the weaving patterns of
the Native American baskets in The Ahwahnee's lobby. Gilded oak
leaves provide a natural counterpoint to the ornaments, and a clus-
ter of them make a unique tree topper.

To make the gilded oak-leaf ornaments, cover fresh leaves with
white acrylic paint. Next, apply acrylic metallic gold spray paint to
each leaf and let dry. To hang, punch a hole at the stem end.
Thread ribbon through the hole, knot, and then tie to the tree.

Antique Chinese foot tubes filled with flowers and other natural arrangements brighten the many rooms of The Ahwahnee. Pink-and-white amaryllis loom over a poinsettia, azaleas, and a spruce tree (right). Seeded eucalyptus, a pomegranate, a dried orange, pinecones, and pepper berries create a colorful candle ring (below). Opposite: Naturals embellish a 22-foot-long hearth in the Great Lounge (see Resources on page 154 for topiaries). A favorite spot for afternoon tea, this room features wrought-iron chandeliers, hanging rugs, and floor-to-ceiling windows with stained-glass panels fashioned in original Native American designs.

In The Ahwahnee's Mural Room—named for the
painting of Yosemite's flora and fauna that hangs
on the paneled wall—a lush evergreen bears matte-
finished pewter, copper, and champagne-colored
ornaments, as well as wreaths, stars, and spheres
covered in tiny pepper berries (above and opposite).
Pepper berries, which are widely available this time
of year from many florists, make wonderful winter
decorations. See page 89 for instructions on how to
make a pepper-berry star.

PEPPER-BERRY STAR

1 To make this festive pepper-berry star, you will need the pattern on page 156, tracing paper, a pencil, cardboard, clippers or scissors, pepper berries, a hot-glue gun and glue sticks, and fishing wire.

2 Use the tracing paper and the pattern to transfer the star pattern to the cardboard; cut out. Arrange the pepper berries on the star and hot-glue in place.

3 Once the cardboard star is covered with pepper berries, secure them to the star with fishing wire. Make a hanger by wrapping the wire around one point of the star.

Birch-bark containers, above, trimmed with string and naturals provide a suitably woodsy wrap for Christmas (see Resources on page 154). Opposite: A popular pastime in the Mural Room is to sit in front of one of the many floor-to-ceiling windows by the copper-hooded fireplace and to watch the snow fall. A wreath hanging in the window flanked by matching swags and a basket filled with beautiful amaryllis blooms and azaleas add to the Christmas spirit. If visitors decide to venture outdoors, they can use the room's charming French doors.

Abundantly decorated with vintage-style lights, pinecones, and gingerbread cookies, this tree (above and opposite) pays tribute to the acorn. This was the primary food source of the Miwok Indians, who inhabited the Yosemite Valley more than one hundred years ago. (To make the acorn cookies, use the gingerbread recipe on page 143 and order the copper cookie cutter from Resources on page 154.)

The tree brightens a corner of the Winter Club Room, a place where visitors seek relaxation in deep leather chairs and can admire a collection of winter sports photos from the 1920s and 1930s. This room traditionally displays the gingerbread house made by The Ahwahnee's chef during the Christmas season.

Though popular in Europe for centuries, gingerbread caught on in America around the nineteenth century, when settlers brought their many customs and traditions with them. Variations of this favorite treat developed in the different regions of the United States. In fact, America has a greater array of gingerbread recipes than anywhere in Europe, with countless choices in taste and presentation.

Give personality to brown paper packages with assorted felt leaves and acorns (above and opposite). Echoing the woodsy theme of The Ahwahnee, these gift tags are easy to make. Simply trace the desired patterns (see page 157) onto felt and cut out. Next, use an embroidery needle and floss in a contrasting color to blanket-stitch the leaf and acorn edges (see Resources on page 154 and the diagram on page 156); then add straight stitches and French knots, if desired. Consider personalizing them by adding gift recipients' names to the felt shapes with a paint pen or thread.

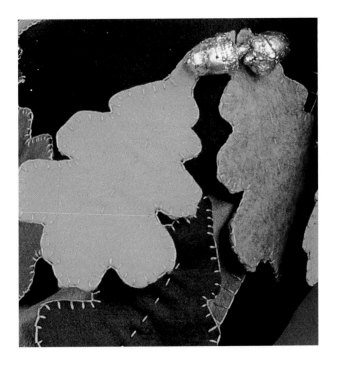

Use the felt shapes to put a festive touch on stockings (above and opposite). To make a stocking, purchase a felt stocking and then outline it with a blanket stitch (see the diagram on page 156), using embroidery needle and floss. (Or you can make your own stocking from felt.) Stitch the felt shapes along the top of the stocking. For a little sparkle, add some gilded acorns.

To make a gilded acorn, brush a coat of white glue onto an acorn; let sit until tacky. Cut "Dutch Metal" gold leaf in an appropriate size and carefully wrap it, gold side facing down, around the acorn; let dry. Burnish the gold leaf with a soft paintbrush; then remove the excess gold.

A birdhouse, a pair of young pine trees, and a basket bursting with bright red amaryllis and greens (left) sits on a table in the hotel's Elevator Lobby, located just outside the Dining Room and the Great Lounge. The basket-swirl mural (below) that hangs over the fireplace in the Elevator Lobby was painted by Jeannette Dyer Spencer, who was the resident artist when the hotel was built. (See Resources on page 154 for birdhouses and topiaries.) Opposite: A doorway is draped with white lights and a garland of manzanita branches, gilded pinecones, and polystyrene spheres covered with twigs and dried citrus peels.

The exterior of The Ahwahnee is just as breathtaking as the interior. The landscape around the hotel—a concrete structure stained to look like redwood, with rock columns and varied levels—includes a view of the towering granite cliffs that surround the Yosemite Valley. Outdoor Christmas decorations enhance the festive atmosphere for visitors taking an afternoon stroll around the grounds. A footed wire basket filled with diminutive evergreens and faux silvered-glass ornaments (above, left) sits outside the hotel's front door. A pair of snow boots filled with tiny trees (above, right) adds a touch of whimsy to a snow scene. Opposite: Christmas trees—ready to be decorated—rest against stone walls of The Ahwahnee.

The blanket of snow that covers the Yosemite Valley and the abundance of natural materials in the area provide the means for another great Christmas decoration: snowmen. The best time to build these symbols of the season is when the temperature is right around freezing, which is when the snow isn't too powdery or slushy. These snow creatures come in all different shapes and sizes—limited only by imagination. A young visitor to The Ahwahnee puts the finishing touches on his winter classic (above). Pinecones and greens gathered from the nearby woods bring the snowman to life. Opposite: A hat and disarming grin gives character to this charming snowman, who offers Christmas ornaments from an outstretched arm. When it comes to decorating these snowy chaps, any materials will do—berries, pinecones, sticks, ornaments, whatever is on hand.

A snowman keeps friendly watch outside of The Ahwahnee. Instead of wearing a traditional top hat or mop, his head is crowned with three branches of leaves. Some sticks and pinecones, gathered from nearby woods, complete his impish look.

YOSEMITE: Wawona Hotel

THE LOCAL MIWOK PEOPLE called the tranquil meadow *Pallachun*—or "a good place to stop." Since the mid-nineteenth century, Yosemite National Park's Wawona Hotel has been hosting visitors at the site, and judging by its year-round popularity, it indeed remains a very good place to stop. One of the oldest mountain resort hotels, the Wawona has long verandas furnished with Adirondack chairs, generous expanses of sloping lawn, and guest rooms decorated with period pieces.

At Christmastime the Wawona takes on a holiday air. The hotel is made bright with arrangements of potted flowers draped in garlands and wreaths of natural mountain greenery (all brought in from the outside, since regulations do not allow the removal of any plants from the park). The fresh scent of evergreen branches mingles with the smell of wood smoke from the hotel's natural stone fireplaces; in the lobby lounge, guests gather by the snow-covered windows to play cards or to write letters. Like Christmas itself, the charming Wawona Hotel is layered in tradition, an ever-changing blend of old and new.

Old-fashioned candies make an inviting display on a polished desk at the Wawona Hotel (above). Opposite: In keeping with the spirit of Yosemite, Christmas decorations at the Wawona employ natural materials. Following pages: Garlands and lights drape the Wawona Hotel for Christmas.

California sugar pinecones—which can grow more than a foot in length—combined with miniature pinecones and pepper berries (above), punctuate the cedar garlands that grace the doorways of The Wawona's main lounge (opposite). The oldest structure on the property, this Victorian-style main building was constructed in 1879. The main dining room was annexed to the cottage in 1918, the same year that the golf course and the swimming pool opened.

White candles, silver pinecone ornaments, and silver pots filled with
Christmas greens and white flowers
decorate the mantel in the Clark
Cottage (above and opposite). A bay
wreath hangs above the mantel arrangement. A garland of miniature pinecones, anchored with sugar cones,
cedar, and pepper berries, drapes across
the stone fireplace. The sugar cone
groupings at the ends echo the cedar
doorway garlands. White azaleas,
pinecones, pepper berries, and moss fill
a basket sitting on a table beside the
fireplace.

To Make and to Give

THE DELIGHTFUL PAUSE YOU take at Christmas—when the demands and the routines of the rest of the year are suspended—is a wonderful time to reacquaint yourself with the quiet pleasures of home. Whether greeting returning family and visiting friends or simply settling in with the people you see every day, you cherish home as the heart of the holiday season. The tree is decorated, the front door is hung with a bright wreath, the silver is polished, and the cupboards and freezer are full of holiday treats. So relax and enjoy!

Projects and pursuits that often get swept aside in the rush of daily living take on new appeal during cozy stay-at-home holidays: a communal jigsaw puzzle set up on a card table, a bright scarf knitted in quiet moments by the fire, a batch of cookies scenting the whole house. Neighbors, who are perhaps no more than nodding acquaintances most of the year, have time to share a cup of tea, to exchange handmade presents or gifts from the kitchen. As life slows down to a leisurely pace, your home may seem an island in time, as exciting as the most distant destination, yet comfortable and familiar.

A generous wreath of cedar (above) is decorated with cotton pods, popcorn berries, pinecones, boxwood, and miniature fresh apples. Opposite: Holidays at home are a time to exercise your creativity and put your own unique stamp on Christmas traditions, as with this painted wooden snowman, whose charm will never melt away.

The most popular styles of yellowware—which is named for the light yellow-colored clay used to create it—were made in the nineteenth and early twentieth centuries. Embossed yellowware (above), formed in molds with raised designs, was readily available. Bowls were often sold in sets, in which small bowls would fit into larger ones. Originally made for baking or serving food, a grouping of bowls now holds a display of greens, lemons, pinecones, and apples (opposite).

Yellowware was widely used for practical and aesthetic reasons: It is lighter in weight than stoneware and sturdier than redware, making it useful for baking and serving. Also, there was a wide variety of decorations available, including the popular mocha motif, which features colorful, wavy designs applied with a feather quill or a sponge. Another common treatment was a Rockingham glaze, achieved by spattering a brown glaze onto a piece previously dipped into a clear glaze.

Following pages: Some favorite yellowware pieces include mugs, bowls, creamers, and pitchers.

Winter's varied harvest provides such wonderful shapes, textures, and colors for holiday decorating. A trip to the grocery store or florist will yield an abundance of materials. Bright fruits, such as cranberries and kumquats, combined with pinecones, nuts, and cinnamon sticks (above) add a twist to the traditional color scheme of red and green. Opposite: To make this fragrant garland, drill a small hole in each of several pinecones and cinnamon sticks. Then alternately thread eucalyptus leaves, apples, cinnamon sticks, and pinecones onto a string with a long needle. Knot both ends of the string and attach the garland where desired with raffia ties.

Kumquats, with their thick skins, are ideal for holiday decorating because they usually last several weeks. They add quaint charm to a string of cranberries, pinecones, and cinnamon sticks (above).

The warm color of kumquats brightens a chain of nuts, pinecones, cinnamon sticks, and eucalyptus leaves (below). Opposite: Kumquat bunches hang from a garland of cranberries and nuts.

KITCHEN GIFTS

MAIL-ORDER CATALOGS AND gourmet shop shelves bulge this time of year with exotic holiday treats from around the world. But nothing quite compares with a handmade gift from your kitchen. Whether elaborate or simple, spicy or sweet, home-baked goods convey the warmth of your wishes in a way that nothing else can.

Part of the fun of homemade gifts is in the presentation: bright wrapping paper and colorful ribbons, custom-made cards and labels, and pretty jars, baskets or boxes (keep Christmas in mind as you browse flea markets and yard sales throughout the year). The packages don't need to be sophisticated or fancy to be pleasing—in fact, part of their charm is in their do-it-yourself simplicity. From the pleasure of making to the pleasure of giving, home-cooked gifts are the essence of Christmas. Establish a kitchen tradition, and friends will look forward to the annual arrival of a basket of your cookies or a jar of your jam as a taste of the season itself.

Christmas pleasures include the anticipation of once-a-year holiday fare. Classic creamy eggnog dusted with sprinkles of freshly grated nutmeg (opposite and above) fulfills the fantasy.

HOLIDAY EGGNOG

(PICTURED ABOVE)

MAKES 8 SERVINGS

6 large egg yolks

1 cup sugar

½ teaspoon vanilla extract

¼ teaspoon ground nutmeg

2 cups milk

¾ cup rye or blended whiskey

¼ cup rum

1 cup heavy cream

2 cups heavy cream, whipped

Ground nutmeg

1. Beat egg yolks at medium speed with an electric mixer until thick and lemon colored; gradually add 1 cup sugar, vanilla, and ¼ teaspoon nutmeg, beating well at medium speed.

2. Place milk in a heavy saucepan over medium-low heat. Gradually add egg yolk mixture; cook, stirring constantly with a wire whisk, until mixture reaches 160° (about 20 to 30 minutes). Remove from heat; let cool.

3. Stir in rye, rum, and 1 cup cream. Cover and chill 8 hours.

4. Place chilled mixture in a punch bowl. Fold whipped cream into chilled mixture. Sprinkle with nutmeg.

•NUTRITION INFORMATION PER SERVING—PROTEIN: 5.9G; FAT: 38.9G; CARBOHYDRATE: 30.6G; FIBER: 0.0G; SODIUM: 69MG; CHOLESTEROL: 290MG; CALORIES: 556

BOURBON-GLAZED ALLSPICE POUND CAKE

A SUGAR GLAZE KISSED WITH BOURBON DRIZZLES DOWN THE SHAPELY SIDES OF THIS SPICED SOUR CREAM POUND CAKE.

MAKES 12 SERVINGS

2¼ cups all-purpose flour
1 tablespoon ground allspice
2 teaspoons baking powder
½ teaspoon salt
¼ teaspoon baking soda
¾ cup sugar
½ cup (1 stick) butter, softened
1 8-ounce container sour cream
2 large eggs
¼ cup milk
2 teaspoons vanilla extract
¾ cup unsifted confectioners' sugar
4 teaspoons bourbon

1. Heat oven to 325°F. Grease and lightly flour a 9-inch Turk's head mold or other decorative 9-inch tube pan. In a medium-size bowl, combine flour, allspice, baking powder, salt, and baking soda; set aside.

2. In a heavy-duty electric mixer with paddle attachment, beat ¾ cup sugar and butter on medium speed until light and fluffy. Add sour cream, eggs, milk, and vanilla; beat until blended. Reduce speed to very low; add flour mixture to sour cream mixture and beat just until batter is blended—do not overmix. Spoon batter into prepared pan.

3. Bake 50 to 60 minutes or until a long wooden pick inserted in center comes out clean. Cool cake in pan on a wire rack 10 minutes. Turn pound cake out onto serving plate and cool completely.

4. Meanwhile, in a small bowl, stir together confectioners' sugar and bourbon. If necessary, add water, a drop at a time, to reach spreadable consistency. Spoon glaze over top of cake, allowing it to run down the sides. Set cake aside until glaze dries. To serve, cut cake into 12 wedges.

•NUTRITION INFORMATION PER SERVING—PROTEIN: 4G; FAT: 13G; CARBOHYDRATE: 38G; FIBER: 0.7G; SODIUM: 353MG; CHOLESTEROL: 65MG; CALORIES: 288

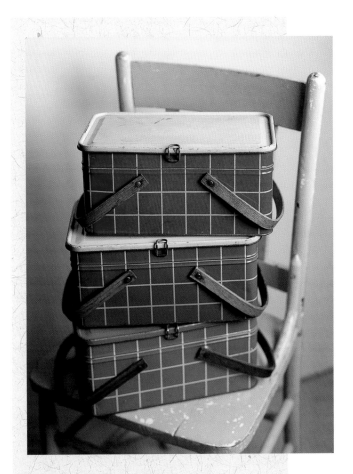

Sometimes the only thing better at Christmas than a package of homemade goodies is the container. Traditional tins make festive wraps for all sorts of treats such as cookies, cakes, breads, and crackers. Once the contents are eaten, the tin becomes a keepsake.

Take as much care in packaging the goods as you do in selecting the tin. Cushion them with materials such as colorful paper shreds, waxed tissues, tinted cellophane, or parchment paper. Pad the container with a few layers before and after you add the contents.

VERMONT CHEDDAR CRACKERS

(PICTURED BELOW AND ON FACING PAGE)

SERVE THESE HOLIDAY-SHAPED CRACKERS
WITH A BOWL OF HEARTY SOUP.

MAKES 23 CRACKERS

½ cup (1 stick) butter, softened

½ cup shredded yellow Vermont Cheddar cheese

1¾ cups all-purpose flour

½ teaspoon baking powder

¼ teaspoon salt

1 to 2 tablespoons ice water

1. In a heavy-duty electric mixer with paddle attachment, beat butter and shredded cheese on medium speed until well blended. Reduce speed to low; beat in flour, baking powder, salt, and 1 tablespoon water until dough is smooth. Add more water to make dough manageable, if necessary. Wrap and refrigerate dough 30 minutes.

2. Heat oven to 350°F. Grease 2 baking sheets. Between 2 pieces of floured waxed paper, roll out dough to ¼-inch thickness. Using 3-inch holiday-shaped cookie cutters, cut out dough. Reroll scraps and cut out more shapes until all dough has been used.

3. Place cut dough 2 inches apart on greased baking sheets. With a fork, pierce tops of each several times.

4. Bake until edges are golden brown—10 to 12 minutes. Transfer crackers to wire racks to cool completely. Store in an airtight container.

•NUTRITION INFORMATION PER CRACKER—PROTEIN: 1.6G; FAT: 4.9G; CARBOHYDRATE: 7.4G; FIBER: .0.3G; SODIUM: 94MG; CHOLESTEROL: 13MG; CALORIES: 80

GINGER-GINGER COOKIES

(PICTURED ON FACING PAGE)

THESE PRETTY SUGAR COOKIES ARE INFUSED WITH A DOUBLE DOSE OF PEPPERY SWEET GINGER—GROUND AND CRYSTALLIZED.

MAKES 52 COOKIES

COOKIE DOUGH:

1½ cups all-purpose flour
1 tablespoon ground ginger
1 teaspoon baking powder
¼ teaspoon baking soda
¼ teaspoon salt
½ cup firmly packed light brown sugar
½ cup (1 stick) butter, softened
1 large egg
2 teaspoons vanilla extract
½ cup crystallized ginger, cut into ¼-inch pieces

GINGER SUGAR:

3 tablespoons sugar
1 teaspoon ground ginger

1. Prepare Cookie Dough: In a medium-size bowl, combine flour, 1 tablespoon ground ginger, baking powder, baking soda, and salt; set aside.

2. In a heavy-duty electric mixer with paddle attachment, beat brown sugar and butter on medium speed until light and fluffy. Beat in egg and vanilla. Reduce mixing speed to low; beat in flour mixture and crystallized ginger until soft dough forms.

3. Heat oven to 350°F. Prepare Ginger Sugar: In a small bowl, combine 3 tablespoons sugar and 1 teaspoon ground ginger. Spread out on a rimmed dessert plate. Drop dough by rounded teaspoonfuls, several at a time, into Ginger Sugar and roll to coat. Place sugared dough balls, 1 inch apart, on greased cookie sheets.

4. Bake until just firm—12 to 15 minutes. With a pancake turner, transfer cookies to wire racks to cool completely. Store in an airtight container.

•NUTRITION INFORMATION PER COOKIE—PROTEIN: 0.5G; FAT: 2G; CARBOHYDRATE: 7G; FIBER: 0.1G; SODIUM: 40MG; CHOLESTEROL: 9MG; CALORIES: 47

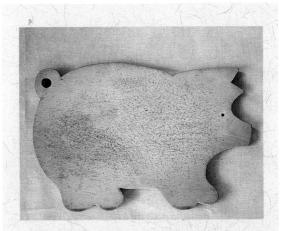

Herald the holidays by indulging in creative serving and gift-giving ideas. Present a tempting batch of special Christmas cookies on your favorite country-style cutting board. Guests will enjoy your casual, homespun approach. To share a savory treat, place a loaf of quick-bread or a nutty cheese ball on a whimsical board and wrap it for a pretty and practical gift idea.

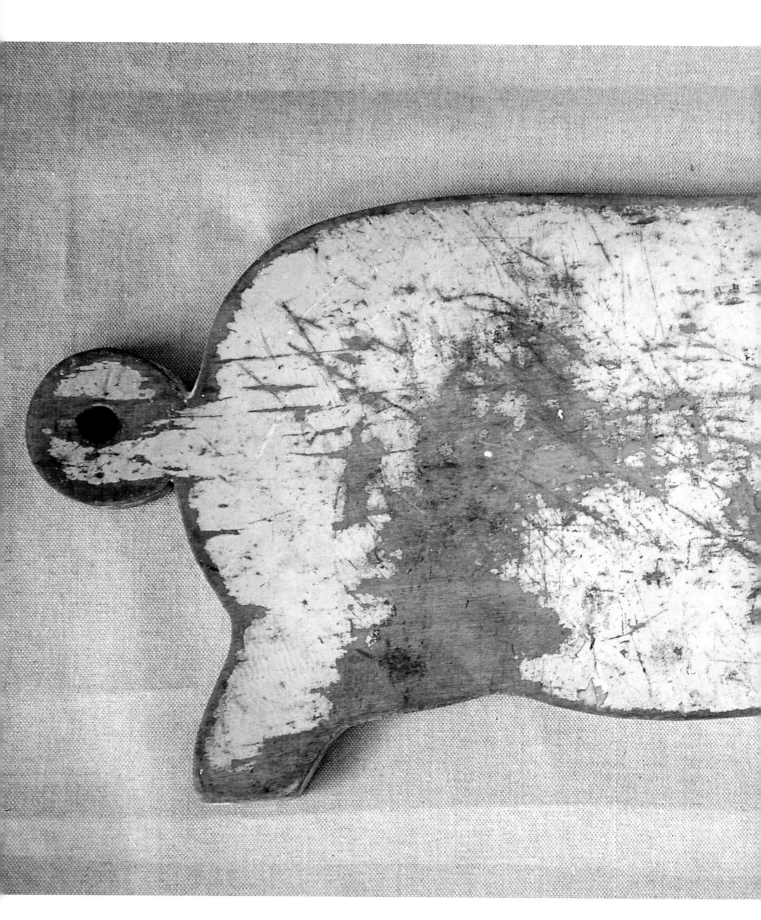

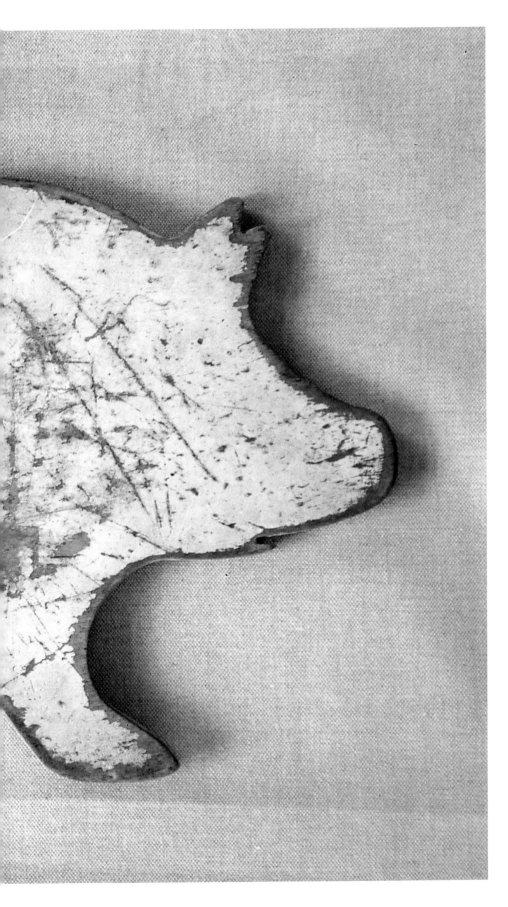

If you can't find just the right cutting board for holiday gift giving and serving, consider making your own. To do this, simply pick a shape you'd like to use as a cutting board and trace it onto tracing paper. (You may need to use a copy machine to make the image the right size.) Place the tracing paper on top of a purchased square cutting board (wood or plastic) and cut it out. Sand the rough edges and use a cloth to wipe away the dust. If you'd like, add a paint finish and coat it with polyurethane.

CHOCOLATE-CHOCOLATE CHIP COOKIES

(PICTURED AT RIGHT AND ON FACING PAGE)

MAKES ABOUT 48 COOKIES

1 12-ounce package semi-sweet chocolate pieces,
   divided
1 cup (2 sticks) butter or margarine, softened
⅔ cup sugar
1 large egg
1 teaspoon vanilla extract
2¼ cups all-purpose flour
1 teaspoon baking soda
1 cup finely chopped walnuts
½ cup shredded or flaked coconut
2 to 3 tablespoons finely chopped pistachio nuts
   (optional)

1. Melt 1 cup semi-sweet chocolate pieces in a small saucepan over very low heat, stirring constantly. Remove from heat; cool.

2. In a heavy-duty electric mixer with paddle attachment, beat butter and sugar on medium speed until light and fluffy. Beat in melted chocolate, egg, and vanilla until fluffy. Beat in 1 cup of the flour and baking soda until smooth.

3. With a spoon, stir in remaining flour, then stir in walnuts, coconut, and ½ cup chocolate pieces.

4. Heat oven to 350°F. Drop dough by rounded tablespoonsful, about 2 inches apart, onto ungreased cookie sheets. Bake until firm—12 to 15 minutes. With a pancake turner, transfer to wire racks to cool completely.

5. Melt remaining ½ cup chocolate pieces in a cup placed in a small saucepan of hot water. Spread a dab of melted chocolate in center of each cookie. Sprinkle with pistachio nuts, if desired. Let chocolate harden before storing cookies in an airtight container.

•NUTRITION INFORMATION PER COOKIE—PROTEIN: 1.6G; FAT: 8.2G; CARBOHYDRATE: 12.6G; FIBER: .8G; SODIUM: 70MG; CHOLESTEROL: 15MG; CALORIES: 125

GINGERBREAD COOKIES

(PICTURED AT RIGHT)

IF YOU'D LIKE TO HANG THESE COOKIES ON YOUR CHRISTMAS TREE, MAKE A SMALL HOLE IN THE TOP OF EACH BEFORE BAKING USING A PLASTIC STRAW. STRING A FESTIVE RIBBON THROUGH THE HOLE AFTER THE COOKIES HAVE COOLED COMPLETELY.

MAKES 4 DOZEN

½ cup (1 stick) butter or margarine, softened
¾ cup lightly packed dark brown sugar
¾ cup dark corn syrup
1 large egg
3¼ to 3½ cups all-purpose flour
1½ teaspoons ground ginger
1 teaspoon ground cloves
¼ teaspoon salt

1. In a heavy-duty electric mixer with paddle attachment, beat butter on medium speed until light and fluffy. Beat in sugar, corn syrup, and egg until well mixed. Reduce speed to low and gradually beat in 1 cup flour, ginger, cloves, and salt.

2. With a wooden spoon, stir in enough of the remaining flour to form a stiff dough. If dough is too firm to work in flour, use hands to mix in flour. Divide dough into thirds. Wrap dough in plastic wrap; refrigerate several hours or until firm enough to shape.

3. Heat oven to 350°F. With a floured rolling pin, roll one-third of dough to ³⁄₁₆-inch thickness on floured aluminum foil or parchment paper cut to fit on a cookie sheet. Place 3-inch cookie cutter on top of dough; cut out cookies and remove trimmings. Allow ½-inch space between cookies.

4. Place foil or paper with cookies onto cookie sheet. Bake cookies until firm—about 8 to 10 minutes. Transfer foil or paper to a wire rack to cool completely. Remove cookies from foil or paper and store in an airtight container.

•NUTRITION INFORMATION PER COOKIE—PROTEIN: 0.9G; FAT: 2G; CARBOHYDRATE: 13.8G; FIBER: 0.3G; SODIUM: 41MG; CHOLESTEROL: 5MG; CALORIES: 75

The time-honored tradition of gingerbread sweets dates back to the Middle Ages when ladies gave gingerbread favors to knights before they engaged in tournament battle. This dense and generously spiced cookie dough can be transformed into anything from plump gingerbread men to fanciful holiday shapes. Tie up your treasures in clear gift bags for at-the-ready favors for your guests.

ALMOND SUGAR COOKIES

(PICTURED ON FACING PAGE)

MAKES 24 COOKIES

Vegetable cooking spray
3 cups all-purpose flour
1 tablespoon baking powder
½ teaspoon salt
1 cup sugar
6 tablespoons butter, cut into pieces
6 tablespoons shortening
3 large eggs, separated
1½ teaspoons almond extract
¼ cup orange juice
1 cup sliced natural almonds

1. Heat oven to 350°F. Lightly coat 2 large cookie sheets with cooking spray. Set aside. Sift flour, baking powder, salt, and sugar into a large mixing bowl. Cut in butter and shortening with a pastry blender or two knives until it resembles coarse meal. Mix in egg yolks.

2. In a heavy-duty electric mixer, beat egg whites and almond extract until soft peaks form—about 3 minutes. Fold whites into dough. Mix in orange juice.

3. Turn out dough onto a lightly floured surface and knead briefly until dough comes together and is smooth—about 2 minutes. Roll out dough into a 9- by 12-inch rectangle about ½ inch thick. Using a fluted pastry cutter or a sharp knife, cut down the 12-inch length of the rectangle to divide the dough into 3 (3-inch-wide) strips. Cut each strip into 4 (3-inch squares). Cut along the diagonal of each square to form 24 triangles.

4. Place cookies on greased cookie sheets and sprinkle almonds over each cookie. Press almonds lightly into dough. Bake until edges are lightly browned—about 7 to 10 minutes. Using a pancake turner, transfer to wire racks to cool completely. Store in an airtight container.

•NUTRITION INFORMATION PER COOKIE—PROTEIN: 3.2G; FAT: 8.9G; CARBOHYDRATE: 13.2G; FIBER: 0.9G; SODIUM: 114MG; CHOLESTEROL: 34MG; CALORIES: 144

NUTMEG SUGAR COOKIES

YOU'LL ENJOY SENSATIONAL BENEFITS FROM THESE NUTMEG-LACED TEA CAKES—THE FRAGRANT AROMA AS THEY BAKE AND THE BUTTERY GOODNESS IN EACH BITE.

MAKES 48 COOKIES

1 cup (2 sticks) butter, softened
1½ cups sugar
2 large eggs
1 (8-ounce) container sour cream
1½ teaspoons vanilla extract
4½ cups all-purpose flour
1 teaspoon baking powder
1 teaspoon baking soda
1 teaspoon salt
¾ teaspoon ground nutmeg
Sparkling white sugar

1. Beat butter at medium speed of an electric mixer until creamy; gradually add 1½ cups sugar, beating well. Add eggs; beat well. Add sour cream and vanilla; beat well.

2. Combine flour and next 4 ingredients; gradually add to butter mixture, beating well. Cover and chill at least 1 hour.

3. Heat oven to 375°F. Divide dough into fourths. Work with 1 portion of dough at a time, storing remainder in refrigerator. Roll each portion to ¼-inch thickness on a lightly floured surface. Cut with a 3-inch cookie cutter; place on ungreased cookie sheets. Sprinkle cookies with sparkling sugar.

4. Bake until lightly browned—about 12 minutes. Cool slightly on cookie sheets. Using a pancake turner, transfer to wire racks to cool completely. Store in an airtight container.

•NUTRITION INFORMATION PER COOKIE—PROTEIN: 1.7G; FAT: 5G; CARBOHYDRATE: 15.4G; FIBER: 0.3G; SODIUM: 129MG; CHOLESTEROL: 23MG; CALORIES: 114

FUDGY PEPPERMINT BROWNIES

MAKES 12 BROWNIES

¼ cup (½ stick) butter or margarine, softened

¾ cup sugar

1 large egg

2 tablespoons water

2 teaspoons vanilla extract

¾ cup all-purpose flour

¼ teaspoon baking powder

⅛ teaspoon salt

⅓ cup cocoa

8 hard round peppermint candy pieces, finely crushed

1 large egg white

1. Beat butter at medium speed of an electric mixer until creamy; gradually add sugar, beating well. Add egg, water, and vanilla, and beat well.

2. Combine flour and next 4 ingredients; add to butter mixture, stirring just until dry ingredients are moistened. Set aside. Beat egg white at high speed until stiff peaks form; gently fold into cocoa mixture.

3. Heat oven to 350°F. Pour batter into a lightly greased 8-inch square baking pan. Bake 25 minutes. Cool in pan on a wire rack. Cut into bars. Store in an airtight container.

•NUTRITION INFORMATION PER BROWNIE—PROTEIN: 2.4G; FAT: 4.8G; CARBOHYDRATE: 23G; FIBER: 0.2G; SODIUM: 87MG; CHOLESTEROL: 19MG; CALORIES: 144

MARBLED BROWNIES

(PICTURED AT LEFT AND ON FACING PAGE)

MAKES 16 BROWNIES

3 ounces unsweetened chocolate

¼ cup (½ stick) butter or margarine

1 (8-ounce) package cream cheese, softened

¼ cup sugar

1 tablespoon cornstarch

1 large egg

¼ teaspoon almond extract

2 large eggs

¾ cup sugar

½ cup all-purpose flour

½ teaspoon baking powder

¼ teaspoon salt

1 teaspoon vanilla extract

½ cup finely chopped walnuts

1. Melt chocolate and butter in a small saucepan over low heat; let cool to room temperature.

2. In a heavy-duty electric mixer with paddle attachment, beat cream cheese until fluffy. Gradually beat in ¼ cup sugar, cornstarch, 1 egg, and almond extract. Beat until smooth; set aside.

3. Wash and dry beaters. Beat 2 eggs in another small mixing bowl until thick. Gradually beat in ¾ cup sugar. Reduce speed to low; beat in chocolate mixture, flour, baking powder, salt, and vanilla. Stir in nuts with a spoon.

4. Heat oven to 350°F. Grease a 9-inch square baking pan. Spread half of chocolate mixture in pan. Pour cream cheese mixture over chocolate layer. Spoon small dollops of remaining chocolate mixture on top. (It will not cover all of cream cheese mixture.) With a spoon, swirl mixtures together slightly to marbleize.

5. Bake until firm—about 40 minutes. Cool in pan on a wire rack 10 minutes. Cut into squares. Cool completely in pan on rack. Wrap in plastic wrap; store in refrigerator.

•NUTRITION INFORMATION PER BROWNIE—PROTEIN: 3.74G; FAT: 14.3G; CARBOHYDRATE: 18.4G; FIBER: 1.2G; SODIUM: 139MG; CHOLESTEROL: 63MG; CALORIES: 208

Pistachio Biscotti

(PICTURED ON FACING PAGE)

PISTACHIO NUTS STUD THESE TWICE-BAKED ITALIAN COOKIES. THEIR SUBTLE, DELICATE FLAVOR AND CRUNCHY TEXTURE MAKE THEM IDEAL FOR DIPPING INTO A WARMING CUP OF COFFEE OR TEA.

MAKES ABOUT 60 BISCOTTI

2 cups all-purpose flour
1 teaspoon baking powder
1 teaspoon baking soda
¾ cup sugar
⅓ cup shelled, unsalted pistachio nuts, coarsely chopped
2 large egg whites
1 large egg
1 teaspoon vanilla extract

1. Heat oven to 350°F. Lightly grease 2 cookie sheets. In a small bowl, combine flour, baking powder, baking soda, sugar, and pistachios.

2. Combine egg whites, egg, and vanilla, whisking until blended. Add to dry ingredients and stir until blended. Place mixture on a lightly floured surface. Knead until well blended. Shape into 2 (15½ by 1½-inch) logs. Place logs on the lightly greased cookie sheets.

3. Bake logs 20 minutes or until light golden brown. Cool logs on cookie sheets on wire racks 10 minutes. Remove logs from cookie sheets and cut crosswise into ½-inch-thick slices. On same cookie sheets, place biscotti, cut side down. Bake until light brown on both sides—about 5 minutes longer, on each side, or until light golden brown on both sides. Cool completely on cookie sheets on wire racks; store in an airtight container.

•NUTRITION INFORMATION PER BISCOTTI—PROTEIN: 1.2G; FAT: .7G; CARBOHYDRATE: 8.9G; FIBER: 0.3G; SODIUM: 48MG; CHOLESTEROL: 5MG; CALORIES: 46

Empty glass cookie jars just seem to beckon the cook for a fresh batch of homemade cookies, especially during the holiday season. Look for jars at flea markets or kitchen shops throughout the year. Any kind of interesting jars will do. Then, when Christmas finally arrives, you'll have some on hand to fill with cookies and give as gifts or share with visitors.

Pewter

The soft gleam of pewter connects us with the daily life of past generations, a time when pewter was used for both everyday and "company best" serving pieces. It is made of an alloy of tin, hardened with just a small amount of copper or lead and brightened with antimony or bismuth. Pewter fashioned into utensils has been discovered in archeological digs dating back to 1500 B.C. The widespread use of pewter began with the Roman occupation of England—when Roman soldiers smelted pewter from tin mined in Cornwall—and grew throughout the next centuries.

Starting in the fourteenth century, European pewter pieces were usually stamped with hallmarks. This practice began as part of strict regulations imposed by The Worshipful Company of Pewterers, an organization of pewter makers dedicated to maintaining high quality standards in their craft. In the Middle Ages pewter was considered fit for royalty: household inventories show that in 1290 England's King Edward I had over three hundred pieces of pewter—and apparently no silver tableware.

Pewter utensils were made in the American colonies as early as the 1630s. Because the raw materials imported from England were heavily taxed and expensive, much American pewter was cast from recycled utensils. The seventeenth and eighteenth centuries marked the high point of pewter in America. All but the poorest households set their tables with a few dishes, spoons, or teapots of pewter. Master craftsmen turned out beautiful and intricate pieces for churches and public institutions. American pewterers, however, could not keep up with the demand, so many of the pewter pieces that graced American tables were imported from England. By 1760, 300 tons of pewter—the equivalent of a million plates or 300,000 tankards—were coming in a year.

By the end of the eighteenth century, pewter's reign was ending; it was replaced with porcelain, which was increasingly mass produced and inexpensive enough for everyday use. Yet, over two hundred years later, pewter—both antique and new—is still appreciated for its humble, forthright beauty and quiet charms. Various pieces are featured on the opposite and following pages.

DELAMATER
HOUSE
INN

Conference Center

Erected
1844

INDEX

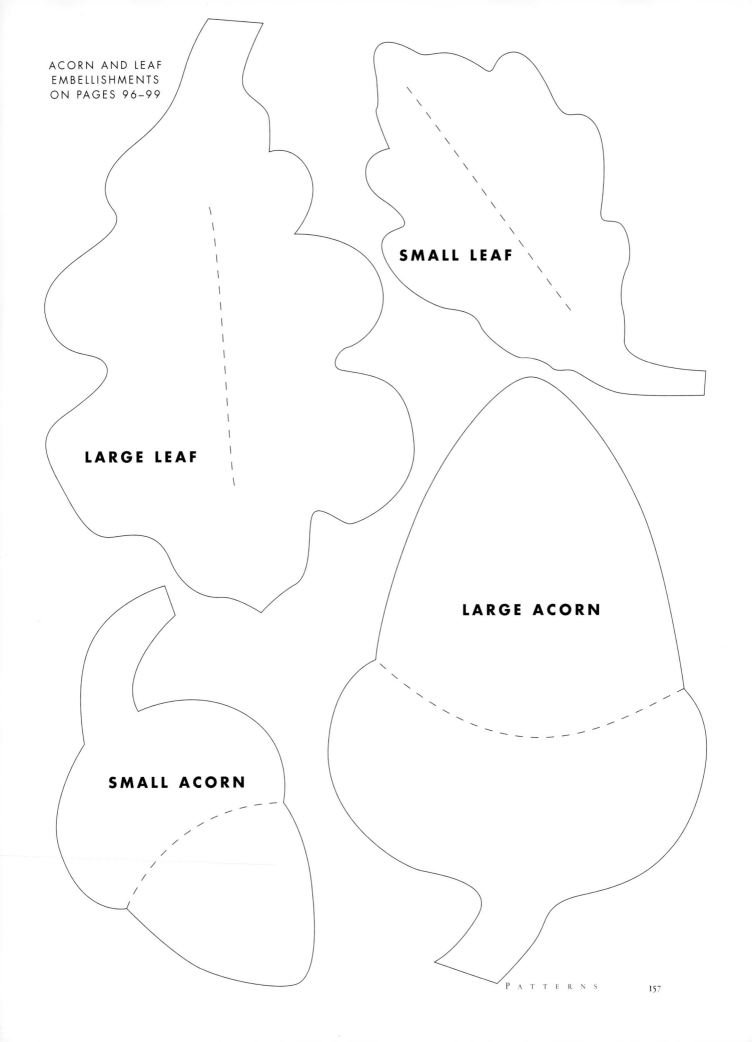

ACORN AND LEAF
EMBELLISHMENTS
ON PAGES 96–99

SMALL LEAF

LARGE LEAF

LARGE ACORN

SMALL ACORN

Patterns

CEDAR STARS ON PAGE 61

PEPPER-BERRY STAR ON PAGE 89

STAR

**BLANKET-STITCH
DIAGRAM**

Linens
John Matouk & Co., Inc.
37 West 26th Street
New York, NY 10010
(212) 683-9242
www.matouk.com

Ornaments
Smith & Hawken
(glass and silver ornaments)
1-800-940-1170
www.smithandhawken.com

Pottery
**Kitchen & Home of the
Hudson Valley**
64 East Market Street
Rhinebeck, NY 12572
(845) 876-6900

Ribbon
C.M. Offray & Son, Inc.
(ribbons)
360 Route 24
Chester, NJ 07930
(908) 879-4700
www.offray.com

Travel
**The Ahwahnee or Wawona
Hotels**
To learn more or make reservations:
Central Reservations
(559) 252-4848
www.yosemitepark.com
National Park Service
1-800-436-7275

Williamsburg
1-800-History
www.colonialwilliamsburg.org

ACKNOWLEDGMENTS

COUNTRY LIVING WOULD LIKE TO THANK THE MANY HOMEOWNERS, DESIGNERS,
AND PHOTOGRAPHERS WHOSE WORK APPEARS ON THESE PAGES.

Photography
Colonial Williamsburg Foundation,
    Williamsburg, VA, pages 14, 18, 19
Keith Scott Morton, pages 68–69, 71, 72–75,
    77, 78–87, 90–93, 95, 97–107

Homeowners and Contributors
Brett Archer
Naomi Arlund
Arlene and Gregory Chiaramonte
Al Gonzalez

RESOURCES

Artisans
Birdhouse Brokerage
(rustic birdhouses, page 101)
P.O. Box 466
Poughkeepsie, NY 12602
1-877-895-1496
birdhous@frontiernet.net
www.birdhousebrokerage.com

Baskets
Basketville
(rustic baskets, pages 70–71)
P.O Box 710, Main Street
Putney, VT 05346
1-800-258-4553
www.basketville.com

Eddie Bauer
(candles and baskets)
P.O. Box 9700
Redmond, WA 98073-9700
1-800-625-7935
www.eddiebauer.com

Lady Slipper Design
(Ojibwa birch baskets and
    boxes, page 90)
315 Irvine Avenue NW
Bemidji, MN 56601
(218) 751-7501

Palecek
(baskets, pages 72–73)
P.O. Box 225
Richmond, CA 94808-0255
1-800-274-7730
www.palecek.com

Candy
Michael's Candy Corner
candycorner@aol.com
www.candycornerusa.com

Cookie Cutters
***Country Living* Cookie
Cutters**
(acorn cookie cutters, pages 92–95)
Small (303236); large (303237); set
of 2 (303238).
1-800-413-9746

Fabric and Thread
DMC Corporation
(embroidery floss, pages 96–99)
(973) 589-0606
www.dmc-usa.com

National Nonwovens
(felt for gift tags and stockings,
    pages 96–99)
1-800-333-3469
www.nationalnonwovens.com

Fresh Evergreens
Forever Green
(preserved evergreen topiaries,
    pages 85 and 101)
20382 Barents Sea Circle
Lake Forest, CA 92630
(949) 768-3005

Gardenworks
(welded topiary forms, pages 78–79)
P.O. Box 216
Markleeville, CA 96120
(530) 694-2515
www.gardenworkstopiary.com

Fresh Plants and Wreaths
**Bloom-Rite Brand® for
Nurseryman's Exchange**
(amaryllis, azaleas, European trees,
    roses)
San Francisco, CA 94103

Knud Neilsen Co., Inc.
(pepper berries, pinecones)
P.O. Box 746
Evergreen, AL 36401
1-800-698-5656

Paul Ecke Ranch
(poinsettias)
P.O. Box 230488
Encinitas, CA 92023-0488
1-800-468-3253

Lights
Kurt Adler/Santa's World
www.kurtadler.com